GENIUS TRANSPORTATION INVENTIONS

FROM THE WHEEL TO SPACECRAFT

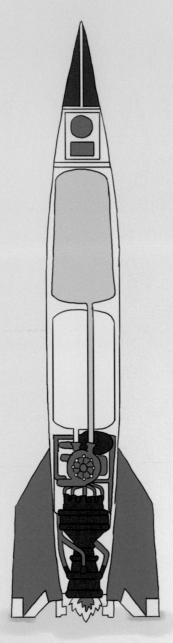

Thanks to the creative team:
Senior Editor: Alice Peebles
Fact Checking: Tom Jackson
Design: www.collaborate.agency

Hungry Tomato®
A division of Lerner Publishing Group, Inc.
241 First Avenue North
Minneapolis, MN 55401 USA

For reading levels and more information, look up
this title at www.lernerbooks.com.

Main body text set in Avenir Next Medium 9.5/12.
Typeface provided by Linotype AG.

Library of Congress Cataloging-in-Publication Data

Names: Turner, Matt, 1964- author. | Conner, Sarah, illustrator.
Title: Genius transportation inventions : from the wheel to
spacecraft / Matt Turner, Sarah Conner.
Description: Minneapolis : Hungry Tomato, [2017] | Series:
Incredible inventions | Audience: Age 8-12. | Audience: Grade 4
to 6. | Includes bibliographical references and index.
Identifiers: LCCN 2016056354 (print) | LCCN 2017006556
(ebook) | ISBN 9781512432091 (lb : alk. paper) | ISBN
9781512450101 (eb pdf)
Subjects: LCSH: Motor vehicles—History—Juvenile literature.
| Transportation—History—Juvenile literature. | Technological
innovations—Juvenile literature.
Classification: LCC TL147 .T87 2017 (print) | LCC TL147 (ebook) |
DDC 629.04/609—dc23

LC record available at https://lccn.loc.gov/2016056354

Manufactured in the United States of America
1-41764-23525-3/7/2017

GENIUS TRANSPORTATION INVENTIONS

FROM THE WHEEL TO SPACECRAFT

by Matt Turner
Illustrated by Sarah Conner

HUNGRY
TOMATO®

Minneapolis

In 2015, a Japanese maglev (magnetic levitation) train reached a record 375 mph (605 km/h) in a test.

CONTENTS

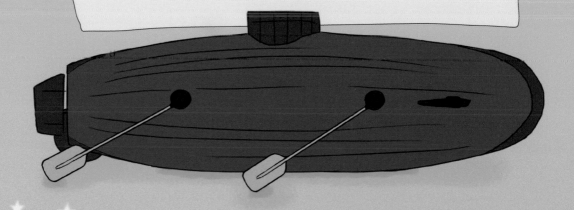

OFF WE GO!

We humans are natural wanderers, but for tens of thousands of years our ancestors moved on foot. They had no other means of transport—not, at least, until they had tamed wild animals. Early humans domesticated the horse, for example, about 6,000 years ago. Many years later, they invented the wheel, which led to carts and chariots. They also harnessed the wind to power sailing vessels so they could cross oceans.

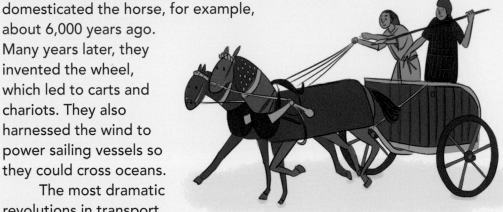

Spoked wheel, 2000 BCE

The most dramatic revolutions in transport have come in the last two centuries, with the development of the steam engine and internal-combustion engine. They powered boats, trains, cars, and aircraft. These inventions brought benefits—speed, comfort—but also problems, such as pollution. Did you know, by the way, that cars were first seen as a clean alternative to horse-drawn transport? That's because the tons of horse droppings in city streets attracted flies, which spread disease. Now, of course, we're choking on exhaust fumes and looking for alternative powers, such as electricity. (Even the Bate car, invented by British chicken farmer Harold Bate in 1971, looks like a healthier idea: it ran on animal droppings!)

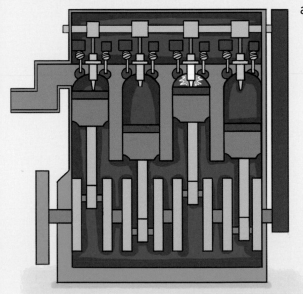

Internal-combustion engine, 1850s

The first aviation pioneers took inspiration from birds, but their flapping flying machines were a disaster. It took the Wright brothers' historic flights of 1903 to unlock the mysteries of manned aviation. Later still, the devastating use of rockets in wartime has led to the peaceful exploration of our final frontier: outer space.

Dugout canoe, 6000 BCE (or earlier)

Model T Ford, 1908

So join us on a journey by almost every craft you can think of, from dugout canoe to spacecraft. And meet the inventors who often risked their reputations—or even their lives—to test new hot air balloons, gliders, parachutes, motorbikes, bicycles, seaplanes, hovercraft . . . and even jetpacks and submarine-planes!

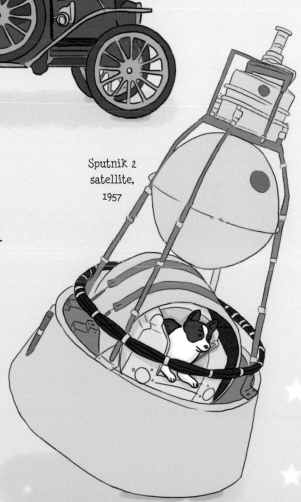

Sputnik 2 satellite, 1957

ON THE ROAD

The invention of the wheel revolutionized transport and technology, but it came fairly late in human history—maybe around 3000 BCE, long after humans had invented spears, flutes, and pottery. In fact the idea came from the potter's wheel. The reason it took them so long is probably because there are no wheels in nature. This was a completely human invention.

PACK ANIMAL

Before we had wheels, we used pack animals. The onager or Asian wild donkey served as a beast of burden in ancient Sumer (modern Iraq).

FIRST WHEEL

The earliest wheels were solid planks, shaped and joined together. Carts like this one appeared in northern Europe in about 2500 BCE. The cart is drawn by domestic cattle.

BENZ PATENT-MOTORWAGEN

In 1885, German inventor Karl Benz (later of Mercedes-Benz fame) produced the three-wheeled Patent-Motorwagen. His wife, Bertha, took it to visit her mom, and on the way she invented brake lining.

ROLLS-ROYCE

The Rolls-Royce 40/50 Silver Ghost appeared in 1907. A car magazine called it "the best car in the world." It was also the most expensive.

MODEL T

American Henry Ford designed his Model T car in 1908. In 1913, he invented the production line: cars were built in a strict sequence—three cars per minute!

SPOKED WHEELS

The Andronovo people, riding their chariots on the Eurasian plains 4,000 years ago, are thought to have invented spokes. Spokes made wheels lighter, bigger, and faster.

STAGECOACH

The coach was invented in Koc (pronounced "kotch"), Hungary. In 17th century Europe, long journeys were made by stagecoach. Early models gave a bumpy ride, but by 1800, coaches were fast and comfy with sprung suspension and brakes.

STEAM ENGINE

Steam engines, used in boats from the 1780s and later in railway locomotives, also began to power road vehicles. The Obedient was a steam carriage made by Frenchman Amédée Bollée in 1875.

HIPPOMOBILE

In the late 1850s, Étienne Lenoir of Belgium invented a gas-powered engine and later used it in his Hippomobile (meaning "horse car," not "hippo car"). Its top speed was 1.8 mph (3 km/h)—slower than walking pace.

> Need a push?

Volkswagen means "people's car." By 2003, more than 21 million Beetles had been sold.

> Hmm, what shall I call it?

BEETLE

Porsche of Germany make luxury sports cars. But back in the 1930s, Ferdinand Porsche also designed the very affordable Volkswagen Beetle—named for its bug-like shape.

THE IC ENGINE

The internal combustion (IC) engine is fueled by gasoline, diesel or petroleum gas. Fuel explosions in the cylinders give out energy, which creates movement to turn the wheels. The IC engine appeared over 150 years ago with many improvements added since.

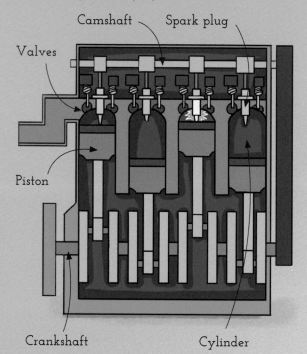

Camshaft

Spark plug

Valves

Piston

Crankshaft

Cylinder

THE FOUR-STROKE CYCLE

1. Fuel/air mix enters cylinder.

2. Piston rises, squeezing fuel/air mix.

3. Spark plug ignites fuel, forcing cylinder down.

4. Piston returns, pushing exhaust (burned gas) out.

CARBURETOR

Fuel is vaporized inside the carburetor (right), which works a bit like an old-fashioned perfume spray. The fuel mist then enters the cylinder heads, where it is ignited by the spark plugs. The first effective carburetors were invented in the 1880s.

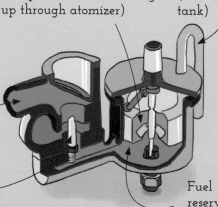

Float (presses on fuel, forcing it up through atomizer)

Fuel intake (from fuel tank)

Fuel vapor (to cylinders)

Atomizer jet (turns fuel from a liquid into vapor)

Fuel reservoir

GAS ENGINE

Remember Étienne Lenoir and the hippo car? This is his 1850s engine. The fuel was coal gas, which in those days was used for street lighting. But around that time, we began converting crude oil into paraffin, kerosene, and gasoline. Gasoline became the preferred engine fuel.

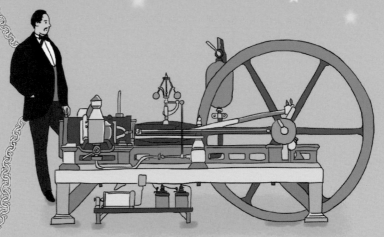

I shall call it... Diesel!

DIESEL ENGINE

From 1892-1897, German Rudolf Diesel invented and improved the engine that bears his name. His first diesel engine was seven times more efficient than steam engines. It produced more power from less fuel.

A V8 engine has eight cylinders. They are arranged in a V-shape, with two blocks of four.

V8 ENGINE

Frenchman Léon Levavasseur invented the V8 engine in 1902, naming it the Antoinette (after the daughter of his sponsor). It was mostly used in planes. This 1905 Darracq racing car had a 22.5-liter V8. It broke the land speed record!

Va... Va... Vrooooom!

ON TWO WHEELS

It's hard to imagine a world without bikes, isn't it? But they were only invented about 200 years ago. The first "bone-shakers" were wood and iron and very hard on the bum. Motorbikes, too, began as very crude machines around 150 years ago.

DRAISINE

The wooden *Draisine* of 1817 was named after its German inventor, Karl von Drais. It had no pedals, so he called it a *running machine*.

VELOCIPEDE

The French Michauline, or velocipede, of the 1860s was designed by Pierre Lallement and Pierre Michaux. It had no tires, but the seat was sprung.

PETROL CYCLE

Englishman Edward Butler invented the three-wheeled Petrol Cycle in 1884. But its top speed of 10 mph (16 km/h) excluded it from some areas; the city speed limit was 2 mph (3 km/h)!

REITWAGEN

The Reitwagen, made by Gottlieb Daimler and Wilhelm Maybach in 1885, was the first true motorcycle. But its seat caught fire. Ouch!

EARLY MOTORBIKE

Hildebrand & Wolfmüller, Germany, 1894—one of the first reliable motorbikes

TRIUMPH

The Triumph Type H, England, 1915—used by messengers in World War I

Bye guys!

PENNY-FARTHING

The ordinary of the 1870s was also called a penny-farthing because its wheels looked like two coins—one small, one large.

Oops!

SAFETY BIKE

Penny-farthings were very hard to ride, and crashed a lot. They were replaced later by safety bicycles. This is the Rover safety bicycle of 1885, made by Englishman John Starley.

HELMET

The lid that saves lives. After famous British soldier T. E. Lawrence died in a motorbike crash in 1935, doctors began calling for the use of crash helmets. In the United States, racing driver Rory Richter was inspired to launch the Bell helmet brand in the 1950s after a friend died in a crash.

MICHAUX

The Michaux steam-powered bike of 1867 was basically a Michauline bicycle with a steam engine attached.

VESPA

Vespa MP-6 "moped," Italy, 1946—a motor scooter for everyone

HONDA

Honda CB750, 1969— one of the first modern, fast Japanese bikes

THE FIRST BOATS

Since paddling the very first fallen log across a creek, we humans have been steadily improving watercraft design. Sails were first used by the Mesopotamians some 5,000 years ago, but the invention of the triangular lateen sail about 1,800 years ago enabled mariners to put to sea in almost any wind. As shipping evolved, so did sea power and trade.

DUGOAT CANOE

From at least 8,000 years ago, dugout canoes served worldwide as simple watercraft. First, pick a long, straight tree trunk, then chop (or burn) the wood from the center. Now take your oar . . .

Row, row, row your boat...

You guys are oarsome!

EGYPTIAN BARGE

This Egyptian barge, built 4,500 years ago, possibly carried the body of King Khufu to his tomb at Giza. There it was sealed into a pyramid for the dead pharoah to use in the afterlife.

BIREME

Around 800-700 BCE, the Phoenicians invented the bireme, a ship with two banks of oars on each side. Some biremes were used for trade, others for battle. War galleys had a sharp beak for ramming enemy ships.

Beak

AIRCRAFT CARRIERS

Modern aircraft carriers are gigantic in order to allow aircraft to take off. Some have measured up to 1,092 ft (333 m) long and have carried up to 90 aircraft. This ship is painted in dazzle camouflage.

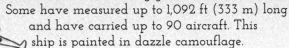

1826 propeller designed by Czech inventor Josef Ressel

PROPELLERS

Ships' propellers were invented in the early 1800s. Paddle wheels are much older. The Romans even had paddle ships powered by cows!

WIND POWER

The caravel was a fifteenth-century Portuguese ship whose triangular lateen sails allowed it to sail in almost any wind direction. This example is the *Matthew*, in which explorer John Cabot crossed the Atlantic in 1497.

GIANT JUNKS

From 1405 to 1423, Chinese traders and explorers mounted sea expeditions as far west as Africa. Under the command of Admiral Zheng He, they sailed in huge fleets of sailing ships known as junks, some 400 ft (122 m) long—among the largest wooden ships ever built. They were often called treasure ships.

15

WATER WONDERS

Why travel on the water when you can go under it? The history of the submarine dates back 400 years—but you wouldn't want to try some of those ancient leaky tubs! Or perhaps a hovercraft is what really floats your boat?

OUTBOARD MOTOR

This 1902 French outboard motor made steering tricky—like using a giant eggbeater! The first serious outboard was made in 1907 by Norwegian-born Ole Evinrude.

HOVERCRAFT

In 1959, Christopher Cockerell crossed the English Channel in his first full-size hovercraft, the SR.N1. His design borrowed ideas from hovercraft research dating back to the 1870s.

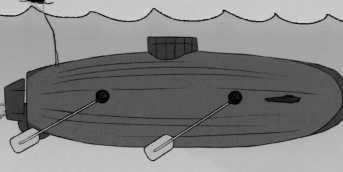

SUB WITH OARS

Cornelius Drebbel was a brilliant Dutchman whose many inventions included a submarine with oars. In 1624, he showed his latest sub to King James I of England and even took the monarch for a ride in the River Thames!

TURTLE

In 1775, American David Bushnell designed the *Turtle*, a one-man submarine. He wanted to use it to place explosives secretly on British ships during the Revolutionary War.

I've sunk so low, solo...

GROUND EFFECT

Ground effect vehicles (GEVs) float several meters above water on a cushion of trapped air. This huge Lun GEV, built in Russia in the 1960s, measured over 300 ft (90 m) long. It was unstable, though, so the idea didn't really "take off."

JETBOATS

Jetboats were invented by New Zealander Bill Hamilton in the 1950s. The engine scoops up water from below and pumps it out the back to push the boat forward.

HOLLAND 1

This is the British Royal Navy's *Holland 1* submarine from 1901 designed by Irish engineer John Holland. She sank off the British coast in 1913 while being towed and was lost. In 1983, she was recovered and restored for museum display.

Holland 1 measured nearly 64 ft (20 m) long and was armed with one torpedo tube.

RAIL TRAIL

Powerful, high-pressure steam engines, invented in the 1800s, soon found their way onto the railways—although the earliest locomotives were very slow puffers! Since then, diesel and electric locomotives and even magnetic levitation trains have drawn the railway into the modern era, providing us with fast, smooth mass transport.

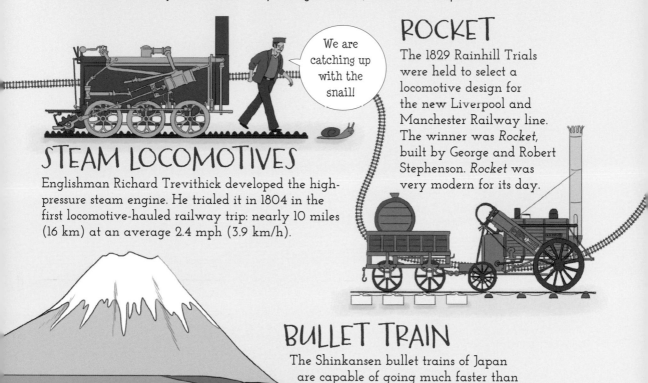

We are catching up with the snail!

ROCKET

The 1829 Rainhill Trials were held to select a locomotive design for the new Liverpool and Manchester Railway line. The winner was *Rocket*, built by George and Robert Stephenson. *Rocket* was very modern for its day.

STEAM LOCOMOTIVES

Englishman Richard Trevithick developed the high-pressure steam engine. He trialed it in 1804 in the first locomotive-hauled railway trip: nearly 10 miles (16 km) at an average 2.4 mph (3.9 km/h).

BULLET TRAIN

The Shinkansen bullet trains of Japan are capable of going much faster than their 200 mph (320 km/h) speed limit. In China, maglev (magnetic levitation) trains float on a magnetic field at speeds of up to 270 mph (430 km/h).

An American diesel-electric of the 1920s, made by General Electric

DIESEL-ELECTRIC

Diesel-electric (DE) locomotives use a diesel engine to power a generator, which drives the electric motor that moves the train. When DEs replaced smoky old steam trains in city areas, it helped keep laundry clean!

ELECTRIC TRAIN

In 1879, German inventor Werner von Siemens built this little electric train—the world's first. (The next year, he built the first electric elevator and, the year after that, the first electric tramway in Berlin.)

METROPOLITAN LINE

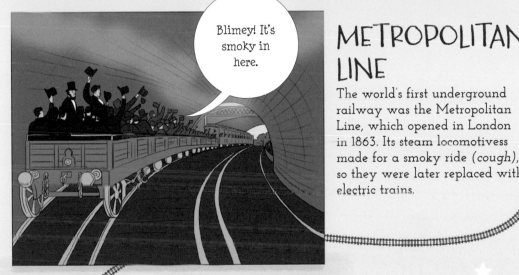

The world's first underground railway was the Metropolitan Line, which opened in London in 1863. Its steam locomotivess made for a smoky ride (cough), so they were later replaced with electric trains.

MALLARD

The British *Mallard*, designed by Sir Nigel Gresley in 1938, still holds the world steam speed record of just over 125 mph (202 km/h). Its beautiful streamlining creates a sleek, slippery shape, keeping wind resistance low.

FIRST FLIGHT

You look at the birds and you want to fly too, right? You're not the first. The earliest attempts go back as far as ancient China. But it was the development of hot-air balloons just over two centuries ago and, much later, the dawn of powered, controlled flight, that turned human dreams of flight into a reality.

CHINESE KITE

As many as 3,000 years ago, Chinese aviators flew strapped to big kites. Later, sailors would send manned kites up into the air to test the prospects of a good voyage.

Hey, you down there... don't let go of that string!

LEONARDO'S MACHINE

The Italian artist-genius Leonardo da Vinci (1452–1519) invented a flying machine inspired by bats and birds, though he never actually built it. (He also invented helicopters—on paper, at least!)

FLOATPLANE

Floatplanes, or seaplanes, are aircraft that can take off from water, and land on it too. They date from 1905, when French aircraft pioneer Gabriel Voisin piloted a float-glider over the River Seine. It was towed by a speedboat.

HOT-AIR BALLOON

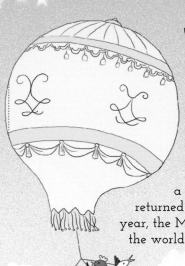

France, September 19th, 1783: the two Montgolfier brothers launch a hot-air balloon carrying a sheep, a duck, and a rooster. The animals returned safely. Later that year, the Montgolfiers launched the world's first manned flights.

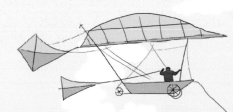

Baa... ooh-ah!

GAS BURNER

The Montgolfiers lit a fire under their balloons to lift them. In 1955, American Ed Yost introduced the on-board gas burner. In 1978, Yost's *Double Eagle II* made the first balloon crossing of the Atlantic Ocean.

GLIDER

British inventor George Cayley sent a glider up in 1853 piloted by one of his servants (who, luckily, came down again unharmed).

ZEPPELIN

This huge airship, which first flew in July 1900, was named after its German inventor, Count Ferdinand von Zeppelin. His first Zeppelin, the *LZ1*, measured 120 ft (128 m)—nearly three times the length of a modern jumbo jet.

AIR POWER

Next time you're in a plane, it'll probably be a comfy jet airliner with in-flight food and maybe movies too. But only a century ago, planes were flimsy craft of stick, string and fabric, with little more than hope and courage to keep them in the air.

JET AIRCRAFT

The first jet planes also appeared in World War II. They were invented by Hans von Ohain in Germany and Frank Whittle in Britain. The Heinkel He178, powered by a von Ohain engine, made the world's first jet flight in 1939.

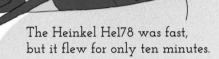

The Heinkel He178 was fast, but it flew for only ten minutes.

Spitfire. Lives up to its name. Better than Shrew, eh.

SPITFIRE

The British Supermarine Spitfire, designed in 1936 by Reg Mitchell, was a famous World War II fighter plane with wing-mounted guns. Mitchell originally wanted to call it "Shrew" or "Scarab," and didn't like "Spitfire." More than 20,000 Spitfires were built and about 50 still fly today.

It flies!

WRIGHT BROTHERS

Wilbur and Orville Wright made the world's first powered flights at Kitty Hawk, North Carolina in 1903. They had begun building gliders, but their first powered plane, *Flyer 1*, carried a 12-horsepower motor.

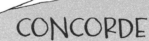

CONCORDE

The beautiful British-French Concorde served as an airliner between 1976 and 2003. It carried up to 128 passengers at over twice the speed of sound. The long nose could be "drooped" on landing so that the pilot could see over it!

EJECTOR SEAT

The ejector seat saves pilots' lives by throwing them from a stricken plane before it crashes. Its inventors include the British company Martin-Baker.

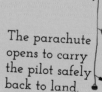

If a plane gets into trouble, the pilot triggers the ejection sequence. First, the canopy opens rapidly.

The seat is quickly blown out by rocket or jet power, lifting the pilot high above the plane.

The parachute opens to carry the pilot safely back to land.

The VS-300 was the first helicopter to use a tail rotor successfully.

Leonardo da Vinci thought of that first!

HELICOPTER

In 1907, Paul Cornu, a bicycle maker, made the first manned helicopter flight, but his experimental craft rose only a few feet. The first truly successful heli was the VS-300, designed in 1939 by Russian-American Igor Sikorsky.

SPACE TRAVEL

If you want to explore space, jets and IC engines are not up to the job. You need a rocket. Large rockets are powerful enough to escape Earth's gravity and carry all their own fuel and oxygen. Space travel is only a few decades old, but it was predicted much earlier by scientists and science fiction fantasy writers.

CHINESE ROCKET

Basic rocket science is this: the engine exhaust pushes backwards to push the rocket forwards. The Chinese grasped this when they invented gunpowder.

MEN ON THE MOON

During the Apollo 15 mission (1971), US astronauts David Scott and Jim Irwin spent three days on the Moon. They traveled the surface in this electric Lunar Roving Vehicle (LRV).

Back in 1903, Tsiolkovsky predicted the use of multi-stage rockets with disposable booster sections.

ROCKET SCIENCE

Russian Konstantin Tsiolkovsky (1857–1935) worked out a lot of the tricky math in rocket science. Although he himself never built a rocket, his work was an inspiration for later pioneers in Germany and the United States.

LIQUID-FUEL ROCKET

On March 16, 1926, American scientist Robert Goddard launched the world's first liquid-fuel rocket. It rose to 41 ft (12 m), then crash-landed in his Aunt Effie's cabbage patch. But he had made history.

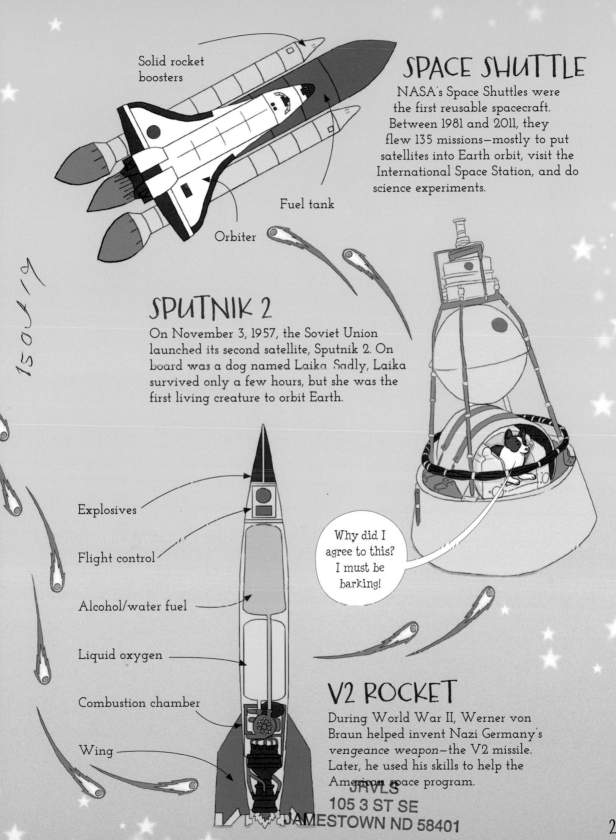

SPACE SHUTTLE

NASA's Space Shuttles were the first reusable spacecraft. Between 1981 and 2011, they flew 135 missions—mostly to put satellites into Earth orbit, visit the International Space Station, and do science experiments.

Solid rocket boosters

Fuel tank

Orbiter

SPUTNIK 2

On November 3, 1957, the Soviet Union launched its second satellite, Sputnik 2. On board was a dog named Laika. Sadly, Laika survived only a few hours, but she was the first living creature to orbit Earth.

Why did I agree to this? I must be barking!

Explosives

Flight control

Alcohol/water fuel

Liquid oxygen

Combustion chamber

Wing

V2 ROCKET

During World War II, Werner von Braun helped invent Nazi Germany's vengeance weapon—the V2 missile. Later, he used his skills to help the American space program.

NAVIGATION

Travelers need to know where they are and where they're going. Finding your way around is called navigating. In early times, this was tricky enough on land but doubly difficult at sea—at least, until the invention of maps, charts, logs, compasses, and other navigational aids.

ERATOSTHENES

HIPPARCHUS

Eratosthenes calculated the circumference of the Earth by measuring shadows cast by the sun. Clever guy!

LATITUDE AND LONGITUDE

Maps have lines of latitude (east-west around the Earth) and longitude (north-south through the poles). The ancient Greeks Eratosthenes and Hipparchus invented latitude and longitude.

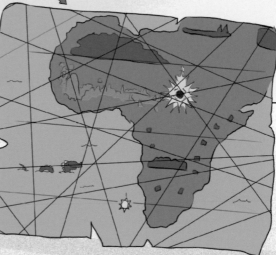

CHARTS

Sailors' sea maps are called charts. Italian mariners of the thirteenth century made the first portulan charts, which showed lines of the compass marking out routes for traders and explorers.

10... 11... 12... 13... How long do I have to count for?

SHIP'S LOG

A ship's log measures speed through water. The earliest one really was a log, which was tied to a rope with knots along its length. Sailors threw the log overboard and counted the knots passing through their hands. That's why a ship's speed is measured in knots.

GPS

These days, mariners have GPS (the Global Positioning System), which uses satellite data to create very accurate electronic charts. The US Department of Defense invented GPS and "switched it on" in 1995.

SEA WATCH

If you could keep time at sea, you could work out your position. This H4 sea watch from 1761 had taken English clockmaker John Harrison six years to make. Captain James Cook took an H4 watch on his famous voyages to the Pacific.

Harrison's watches were very expensive—roughly one-third of the total cost of outfitting a ship!

!?

QUADRANT

Sailors have long used the stars to navigate by. This eighteenth-century seaman is using a Davis quadrant to look back at the sun and measure its angle.

FIRST COMPASS

The ancient Chinese invented the compass: a magnetite pointer on a bronze plate. By the tenth century they'd worked out how to magnetize needles, making better compasses that helped their trading ships navigate at sea.

THIS BABY WON'T FLY!
(TRANSPORTATION MISTAKES)

CAR-RRAZY

The first "car" was a giant, steam-powered three-wheeler designed by French engineer Nicolas-Joseph Cugnot in 1769—well over a century before the first sensible cars took shape. Nick-Joe also had the world's first car crash when his mad invention smashed into a wall in 1771. Not surprising when you consider it had no brakes . . .

The craziest idea for a car? Hmm . . . possibly the Ford Nucleon in 1958 with its on-board nuclear reactor. Luckily, it was never built.

IN A FLAP

In the earliest days of manned flight, many pioneers tried to copy the birds. They built ornithopters—flying machines with flapping wings. The incredible thing is some of them worked . . .

In 1869, Mr W. F. Quinby got a patent for this flapping wingsuit. Thankfully, he never tried to use it.

I'm a bird!

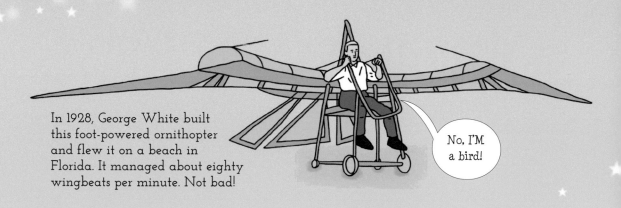

In 1928, George White built this foot-powered ornithopter and flew it on a beach in Florida. It managed about eighty wingbeats per minute. Not bad!

No, I'M a bird!

MASH-UPS

"Know thyself," the ancient Greeks warned us. But clearly some people didn't listen. Just look at these mixed-up craft that don't know whether to sink, swim, drive, or fly.

In 1936, Soviet engineering student Boris Ushakov designed this flying submarine, supposedly capable of 115 mph (185 km/h) in the air and 3 mph (5.5 km/h) in the water. His bosses finally gave it a test run in 1947. It didn't work.

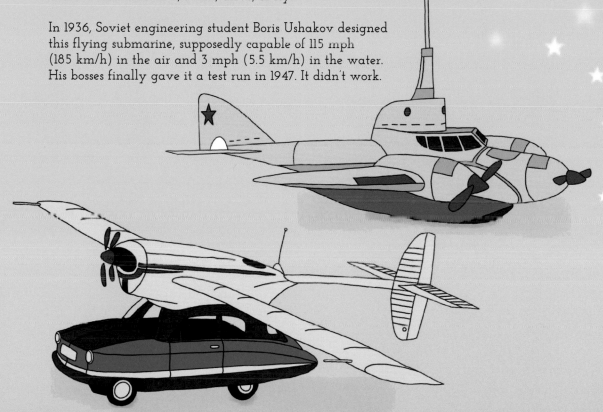

The Convair Model 118 was, as you can see, a car-plane. When the test pilot took it up in November 1947, he forgot to check the fuel, and it ran out of gas, forcing a crash landing. They flew it again in January, but by then Convair had lost interest, and the idea never "got off the ground."

WANNA FLY?

These days, daredevils fly solo using hang gliders, microlights, and wingsuits. They make it look easy, even safe . . . but in days gone by there have been a lot of misguided efforts to invent the perfect personal flight gear.

CHINESE ROCKETS

In Chinese legend, a brave space pioneer named Wan Hu tied rockets to his chair and lit them. One account says he flew, but another says there was a huge explosion: "When the smoke cleared, Wan and the chair were gone, and were never seen again."

WINGSUIT

In 1912, tailor-inventor Franz Reichelt created a wingsuit, which he hoped would work like a parachute. To test it, he leapt off the Eiffel Tower in Paris . . . and fell to his death.

Short and sweet

JETPACK

Fancy your own jetpack? Back in the 1950s, the Bell Company of America invented this rocket belt—but it flew for only twenty seconds.

GLENN MARTIN

Since 1981, New Zealander Glenn Martin has been working on a jetpack. It works . . . but it costs more than $100,000.

WINGPACK

Swiss pilot Yves Rossy also designs jet wingpacks that fly at up to 189 mph (300 km/h). In 2008, he flew across the English Channel in just 13 minutes.

HILLER VZ-1

Designed in the mid-1950s for the US Army, the Hiller VZ-1 Pawnee was the brainchild of aircraft engineer Charles Zimmerman. But the Pawnee was small and slow, and its power was puny, so it only rose up to about 10 m (32 ft).

INDEX

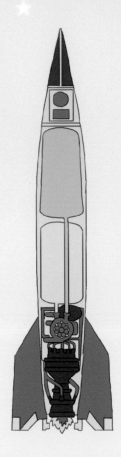

The Author

British-born Matt Turner graduated from Loughborough College of Art in the 1980s, since then he has worked as a picture researcher, editor, and writer. He has authored books on diverse topics, including natural history, earth sciences, and railways, as well as hundreds of articles for encyclopedias and partworks, covering everything from elephants to abstract art. He and his family currently live near Auckland, Aotearoa/New Zealand, where he volunteers for the local Coastguard unit and dabbles in art and craft.

The Illustrator

Sarah Conner lives in the lovely English countryside, in a cute cottage with her dogs and a cat. She spends her days sketching and doodling the world around her. She has always been inspired by nature and it influences much of her work. Sarah formerly used pens and paint for her illustrations, but in recent years she has transferred her style to the computer as it better suits today's industry. However, she still likes to get her watercolors out from time to time and paint the flowers in her garden!